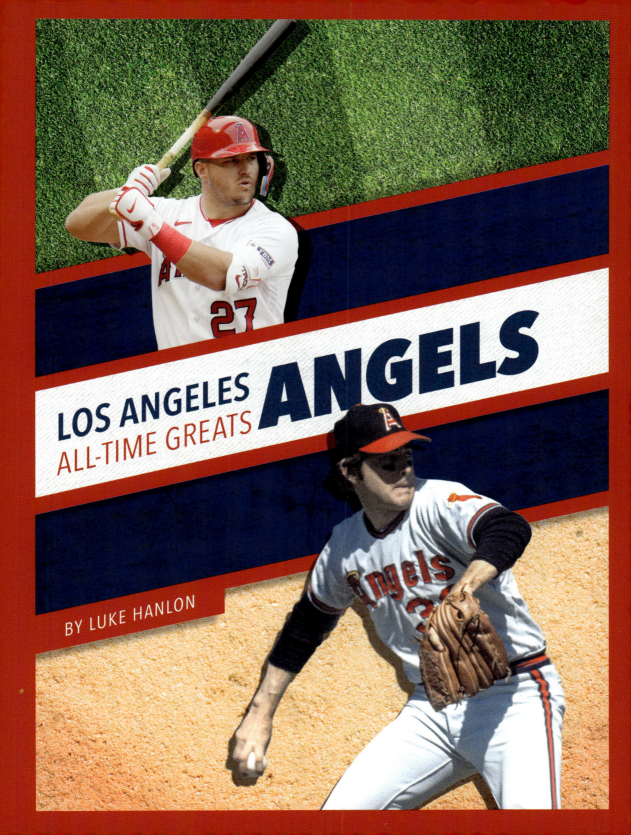

LOS ANGELES ANGELS
ALL-TIME GREATS

BY LUKE HANLON

Copyright © 2024 by Press Room Editions. All rights reserved. No part of this book may be used or reproduced in any manner whatsoever, including internet usage, without written permission from the copyright owner, except in the case of brief quotations embodied in critical articles and reviews.

Book design by Jake Slavik
Cover design by Jake Slavik

Photographs ©: Marcio Jose Sanchez/AP Images, cover (top), 1 (top); David Durochik/AP Images, cover (bottom), 1 (bottom); Bettmann/Getty Images, 4; Photo File/Hulton Archive/ Getty Images, 7; Ron Vesley/MLB Photos/Getty Images Sport/Getty Images, 9; Stephen Dunn/ Getty Images Sport/Getty Images, 10; John Cordes/Icon Sportswire/AP Images, 13; John Hayes/AP Images, 14; Kirby Lee/Getty Images Sport/Getty Images, 16; Sean M. Haffey/Getty Images Sport/Getty Images, 19; Steph Chambers/Getty Images Sport/Getty Images, 21

Press Box Books, an imprint of Press Room Editions.

ISBN
978-1-63494-798-5 (library bound)
978-1-63494-818-0 (paperback)
978-1-63494-856-2 (epub)
978-1-63494-838-8 (hosted ebook)

Library of Congress Control Number: 2023912099

Distributed by North Star Editions, Inc.
2297 Waters Drive
Mendota Heights, MN 55120
www.northstareditions.com

Printed in the United States of America
012024

ABOUT THE AUTHOR
Luke Hanlon is a sportswriter and editor based in Minneapolis.

TABLE OF CONTENTS

CHAPTER 1
ORIGINAL ANGELS 5

CHAPTER 2
WORLD CHAMPIONS 11

CHAPTER 3
VALUABLE TALENT 17

TIMELINE 22

TEAM FACTS 23

MORE INFORMATION 23

GLOSSARY 24

INDEX 24

FREGOSI
11

CHAPTER 1
ORIGINAL ANGELS

The Los Angeles Angels played their first Major League Baseball (MLB) season in 1961. The Angels struggled to find success right away in the American League (AL). Even so, fans loved their players.

Infielder **Jim Fregosi** quickly became a fan favorite. He was one of the team's first expansion draft picks in 1961. Fregosi developed into a consistent star for the Angels. He made six All-Star teams in 11 seasons with Los Angeles. On July 28, 1964, Fregosi became the first Angels player to hit for the cycle.

That year, starting pitcher **Dean Chance** developed into a star as well. The 23-year-old righty led MLB in wins, earned run average (ERA), and shutouts. Chance won the Cy Young Award in 1964. That meant he was the best pitcher in the majors that year.

One of the team's biggest stars arrived in 1972. Starting pitcher **Nolan Ryan** was dominant right away. His fastball, known as the "Ryan Express," struck fear in the eyes of opposing batters.

ANGEL STADIUM

For the team's first five seasons, the Angels shared Dodger Stadium with the Los Angeles Dodgers of the National League (NL). The Angels finally moved into their own stadium in 1966. Angel Stadium was located 27 miles (43 km) southeast of Los Angeles in Anaheim, California. Because the club was moving out of Los Angeles, it changed names to the California Angels.

Oakland Athletics star Reggie Jackson once said batting against Ryan was like "trying to drink coffee with a fork."

Frank Tanana paired up with Ryan in the 1970s to form a dangerous pitching duo. Ryan led the AL in strikeouts in seven of his eight seasons as an Angel. The only year he didn't was 1975, when Tanana led the league.

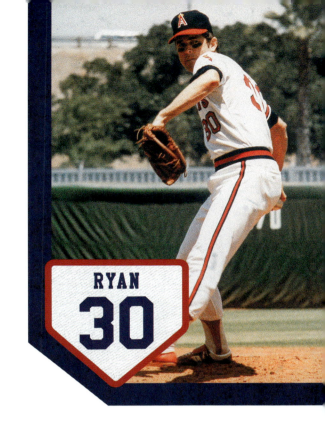

STAT SPOTLIGHT

CAREER STRIKEOUTS
ANGELS TEAM RECORD
Nolan Ryan: 2,416

In 1979, Ryan and Tanana helped the Angels make the playoffs for the first time.

The Angels had plenty of offensive talent as well. Infielder **Bobby Grich** was at the top of his game. Grich had a career-high 30 home runs and 101 runs batted in (RBIs) in 1979. **Brian Downing** was reliable for years with the Angels. When the "Incredible Hulk" left the team in 1990, his name was all over the Angels' record books.

First baseman **Rod Carew** was one of the best hitters of his generation. He was an All-Star six times with the Angels. His arrival just before the 1979 season pushed the team over the top. The Angels won the AL West division. However, they lost to the Baltimore Orioles in the AL Championship Series (ALCS).

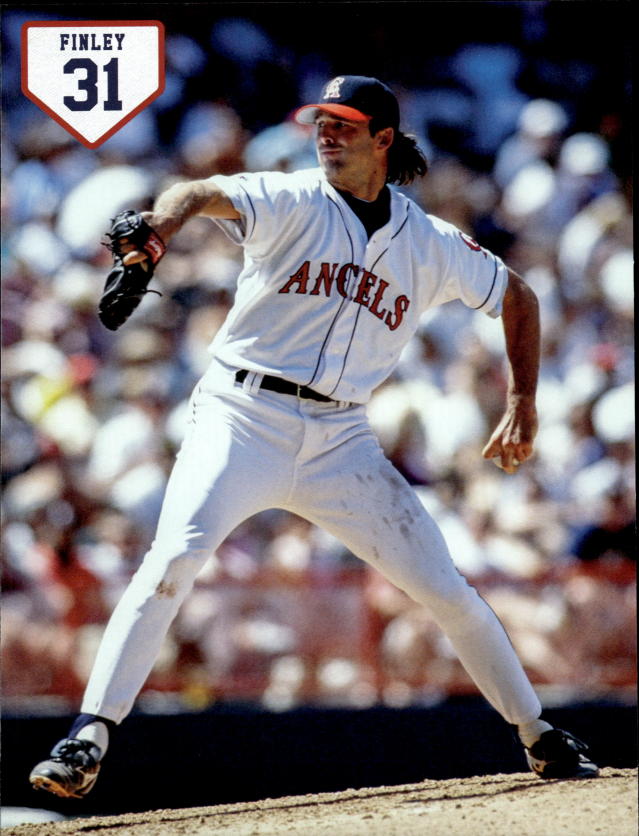

CHAPTER 2
WORLD CHAMPIONS

In the late 1980s and early 1990s, the Angels mostly struggled. One of the bright spots was starting pitcher **Chuck Finley**. The 6-foot-6 (198 cm) lefty rarely missed a start. Finley's 13 complete games led the AL in 1993. In 14 seasons with the Angels, Finley was an All-Star four times.

Tim Salmon broke out in 1993. The right fielder hit 31 home runs and drove in 95 runs on his way to winning the AL Rookie of the Year Award. Salmon hit 30 or more home runs in five different seasons with the Angels.

With more talent, the Angels improved in the late 1990s. Left fielder **Garret Anderson** grew up just north of Los Angeles in Granada Hills, California. He began starting for the Angels in 1995. Anderson was a doubles machine. He led the AL in two-baggers in both 2002 and 2003.

The Angels drafted **Darin Erstad** with the first overall pick in 1995. The versatile outfielder was a good hitter. But he was best known for his fielding. Erstad won three Gold Gloves with the Angels. Those are given to the best defensive player at each position.

Filling out the lineup was slugging third baseman **Troy Glaus**. He led the AL with 47 home runs in 2000. Two years later he had a career-high 111 RBIs as the Angels blasted their way into the playoffs.

The team was helped by two standout rookie pitchers. **John Lackey** threw seven shutout innings in Game 4 of the 2002 ALCS against the Minnesota Twins. The next day,

STAT SPOTLIGHT

SAVES IN A SEASON
ANGELS TEAM RECORD

Francisco Rodríguez: 62 (2008)

the Angels won Game 5 to reach the World Series for the first time. The winning pitcher in that game was rookie reliever **Francisco Rodríguez**. It was one of five games "K-Rod" won in the playoffs.

The Angels faced the San Francisco Giants in the World Series. It went to a seventh game. Anderson smacked a three-run double in the third inning to put the Angels up 4–1. Lackey and Rodríguez sealed the win from there. Glaus's 10 hits, including three homers, won him the World Series Most Valuable Player (MVP) Award.

RALLY MONKEY

The Angels came from behind in 42 different games during the 2002 season. The team believed it had a good luck charm. Late in games, the scoreboard would play a video of a monkey jumping around. The "Rally Monkey" became a huge hit. It even worked in the World Series. In Game 6, the Angels trailed 5–0 but came back to win.

CHAPTER 3
VALUABLE TALENT

After missing the playoffs in 2003, the Angels made a splash before the 2004 season. They signed top free agent **Vladimir Guerrero**. The right fielder could hit for both power and average, ran the bases well, and had a huge arm. He threw out runners from the outfield regularly. Guerrero won the AL MVP Award in 2004 after hitting .337 with 39 homers and 126 RBIs.

Starting pitcher **Jered Weaver** made his MLB debut in 2006. By 2010, Weaver was at his best. He led the AL with 233 strikeouts. The 6-foot-7 (200 cm) righty threw a variety of pitches, which made it hard for batters to counter.

The defense got even better when the team signed **Torii Hunter** in 2008. The center fielder was one of the best defensive players in baseball. Hunter had a knack for robbing home runs from opponents. Those thefts helped him win two Gold Gloves with the Angels.

Hunter eventually moved to right field. He shared the outfield with top prospect **Mike Trout** in 2012. The 20-year-old Trout led the AL in stolen bases and runs scored

MANAGER SCIOSCIA

Mike Scioscia was hired to manage the Angels in 2000. The former World Series–winning catcher quickly improved the team. He led the Angels to their first championship in just his third season. By the time he stepped down after the 2018 season, his 19-year run was the fourth-longest managerial tenure in MLB history.

that season. His play earned him the AL Rookie of the Year Award. Trout only got better from there. He won the AL MVP Award in 2014, 2016, and 2019.

Trout's speed made him a dominant defender and a threat running the bases. His power put fear into opposing pitchers.

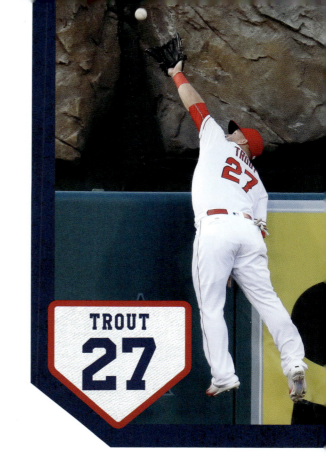

STAT SPOTLIGHT

CAREER HOME RUNS
ANGELS TEAM RECORD
Mike Trout: 350 (through 2022)

For years, Trout was regarded as the best player in baseball.

One elite player wasn't enough. The Angels signed **Shohei Ohtani** out of Japan in 2018. Unlike most players, Ohtani could both pitch and hit at an All-Star level. He won the AL Rookie of the Year Award in 2018. He hit 22 home runs and struck out 63 batters in 51 1/3 innings on the mound.

After some injury-riddled seasons, Ohtani was the AL MVP in 2021. He went 9–2 as a starting pitcher while slugging 46 homers. That same year, Ohtani was the first pitcher, and first Japanese player, to compete in the Home Run Derby. With Trout and Ohtani on the field, Angels fans knew they were watching greatness every game.

OHTANI
17

TIMELINE

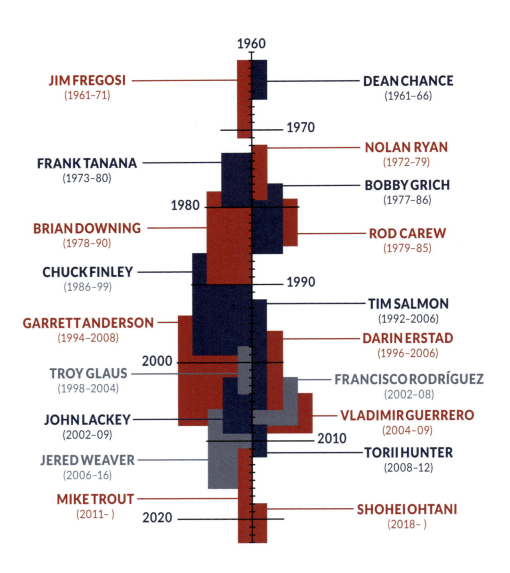

TEAM FACTS

LOS ANGELES ANGELS

Team history: Los Angeles Angels (1961–64), California Angels (1965–96), Anaheim Angels (1997–2004), Los Angeles Angels of Anaheim (2005–15), Los Angeles Angels (2016–)

World Series titles: 1 (2002)*

Key managers:

Gene Mauch (1981–87)
379-332 (.533)

Mike Scioscia (2000–18)
1,650-1,428 (.536), 1 World Series title

MORE INFORMATION

To learn more about the Los Angeles Angels, go to **pressboxbooks.com/AllAccess.**

These links are routinely monitored and updated to provide the most current information available.

*through 2022

GLOSSARY

cycle
When one batter hits a single, a double, a triple, and a home run in a single game.

debut
A first appearance.

elite
The best of the best.

expansion
The way leagues grow by adding new teams.

free agent
A player who can sign with any team.

prospect
A player that people expect to do well at a higher level.

rookie
A first-year player.

shutout
When a pitcher doesn't allow a run.

INDEX

Anderson, Garrett, 12, 15

Carew, Rod, 8
Chance, Dean, 6

Downing, Brian, 8

Erstad, Darin, 12

Finley, Chuck, 11
Fregosi, Jim, 5

Glaus, Troy, 12, 15
Grich, Bobby, 8
Guerrero, Vladimir, 17

Hunter, Torii, 18

Lackey, John, 14–15

Ohtani, Shohei, 20

Rodríguez, Francisco, 14–15
Ryan, Nolan, 6–8

Salmon, Tim, 11

Tanana, Frank, 7–8
Trout, Mike, 18–20

Weaver, Jered, 17